# Powered
## by the Sun

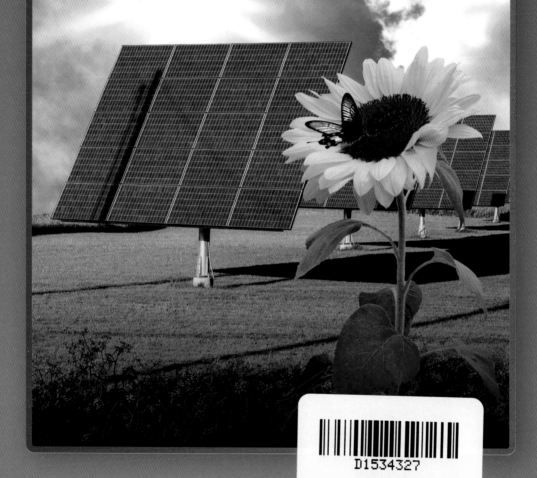

## Joseph Otterman

## Consultants

**Brian Mandell**
Program Specialist
Smithsonian Science Education Center

**Sara Cooper**
Third Grade Teacher
Fullerton School District

**Chrissy Johnson, M.Ed.**
Teacher, Cedar Point Elementary
Prince William County Schools, Virginia

## Publishing Credits

Rachelle Cracchiolo, M.S.Ed., *Publisher*
Conni Medina, M.A.Ed., *Editor in Chief*
Diana Kenney, M.A.Ed., NBCT, *Series Developer*
Emily R. Smith, M.A.Ed., *Content Director*
Véronique Bos, *Creative Director*
Robin Erickson, *Art Director*
Michelle Jovin, M.A., *Associate Editor*
Mindy Duits, *Series Designer*
Kevin Panter, *Senior Graphic Designer*
Smithsonian Science Education Center

**Image Credits:** p.6 © Smithsonian; p.8 Martyn Jandula/Shutterstock; p.9 AFP/Getty Images; p.16 (right), p.17 (middle) Courtesy Radwanul Hasan Siddique; KIT/Caltech; p.18, p.19 (top, middle) NASA; p.19 (bottom) Jean-Marc Giboux/Gamma-Rapho via Getty Images; all other images from iStock and/or Shutterstock.

**Library of Congress Cataloging-in-Publication Data**

Names: Rice, Dona, author. | Smithsonian Institution.
Title: Powered by the sun / Dona Herweck Rice, Smithsonian.
Description: Huntington Beach, CA : Teacher Created Materials, [2020] |
  Audience: K to grade 3. |
Identifiers: LCCN 2018049789 (print) | LCCN 2018052910 (ebook) | ISBN
  9781493868964 (eBook) | ISBN 9781493866588 (pbk.)
Subjects: LCSH: Sun--Juvenile literature. | Solar energy--Juvenile literature.
Classification: LCC TJ810.3 (ebook) | LCC TJ810.3 .R49945 2020 (print) | DDC
  333.792/3--dc23
LC record available at https://lccn.loc.gov/2018049789

## Teacher Created Materials

5301 Oceanus Drive
Huntington Beach, CA 92649-1030
www.tcmpub.com
**ISBN 978-1-4938-6658-8**
© 2019 Teacher Created Materials, Inc.
Printed in Malaysia
Thumbprints.21249

# Table of Contents

# Let the Sun Shine In

Life on Earth exists because of the sun. Living things get energy from it. We get heat and light. We cannot live without the sun.

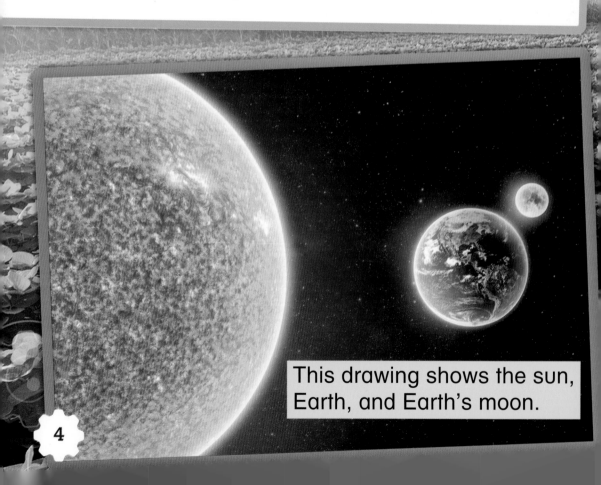

This drawing shows the sun, Earth, and Earth's moon.

The sun also helps people form their best ideas. People study the sun. They test its energy. They watch how living things act in sunlight. Then, they use what they learn to create new things.

The Solar Wall shows how the sun's surface looks.

This scientist checks that these plants get enough sunlight.

# In the Bag

This backpack looks like a normal bag. But it has a **solar panel** in it. The panel gets power from the sun. The power can be used to charge a phone.

# Innovations

Many things have come from studying the sun. People call these things *innovations*. They are new ways of doing things. They make life easier.

This electric car charges under solar panels.

This boat is powered by the sun.

# Sunflowers

Sunflowers face the sun as they grow.  They get more energy that way.

People have set up mirrors like sunflower petals.  The mirrors take in solar power.  They also move to track the sun.

These solar panels are set up like flower petals and move to track the sun.

11

# Electricity

We have learned to gather energy from the sun. We can use it to make steam. The steam spins **turbines**. Their motion makes **electricity**. It all starts with the sun!

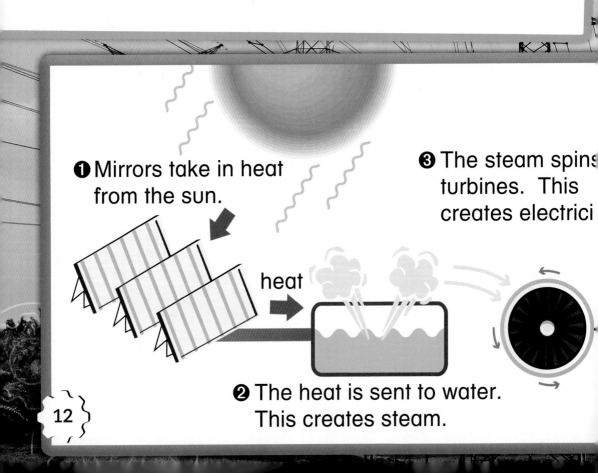

❶ Mirrors take in heat from the sun.

heat

❸ The steam spins turbines. This creates electrici

❷ The heat is sent to water. This creates steam.

❺ Homes receive electricity.

❹ Electricity travels on power lines.

# Solar Oven

The sun gives off a lot of heat. People have learned to cook with it. They just need a solar oven. People can buy or make a solar oven easily. It does not cook quickly, but it does cook well!

This solar oven cooks a pot of rice.

This solar oven is heating water to make coffee.

## Solar Tea

Iced tea drinkers do not need a stove to brew tea. The sun's heat can be used. It works through a closed glass container. Just add tea bags, and the sun brews the tea!

# Butterfly Wings

The rose butterfly is black. Its thin wings grab energy from the sun. Some solar panels are made like the wings. They are thin but mighty. They take in energy with ease.

rose butterfly

This solar panel is made like a rose butterfly wing.

## The Eyes Have It

Some insects have eyes with many **lenses**. There are solar panels made like this. The shapes of the panels let people pack them together. Solar panels like this are strong.

# Under the Sun

People can do many things with energy from the sun. Who knows what great things each new day will bring? Shine on, sun!

This woman checks food she has grown with energy from the sun.

This aircraft is powered by the sun.

This solar panel can bend.

This race car is powered by the sun.

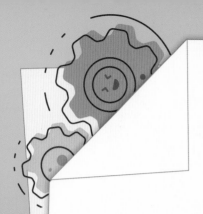

# STEAM CHALLENGE

## The Problem

Your art class is stuck with broken crayon pieces. Your job is to make new crayons by melting and mixing the old bits. You must use the sun to make it happen. What will you do?

## The Goals

- Create a device that will use the sun to melt crayons together.
- Create an area in your device that can hold the crayons.
- Create your device with any supplies. A box, aluminum foil, and plastic wrap might be helpful.

## Research and Brainstorm

What is the best way to melt crayons in the sun? How long does it take for crayons to melt?

## Design and Build

Draw your plan. How will it work? What materials will you use? Build your device. Be careful not to burn yourself!

## Test and Improve

Remove the paper from the crayons. Place the crayons in your device. Place your device outside. Do the crayons melt and blend? Can you make it better? Try again.

## Reflect and Share

How many pieces melted? Do some colors melt faster than other colors? Do the new crayon blends work well?

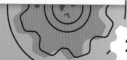

# Glossary

electricity

lenses

**solar panel**

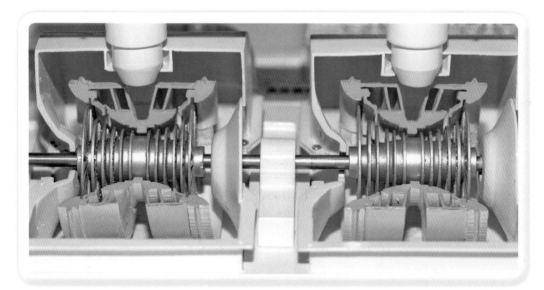

**turbines**

# Career Advice
## from Smithsonian

**Do you want to use the sun to power innovations?** Here are some tips to get you started.

"Think of new ideas that could help people. Then, start trying to build them. If you fail, try again!" — *Susan Tolbert, Curator*

"Creativity and problem solving are important parts of STEAM! If you want to design and power innovations, you must never give up!" — *Mike Hulslander, How Things Fly Gallery Manager*